A SCREAMING WHISPER

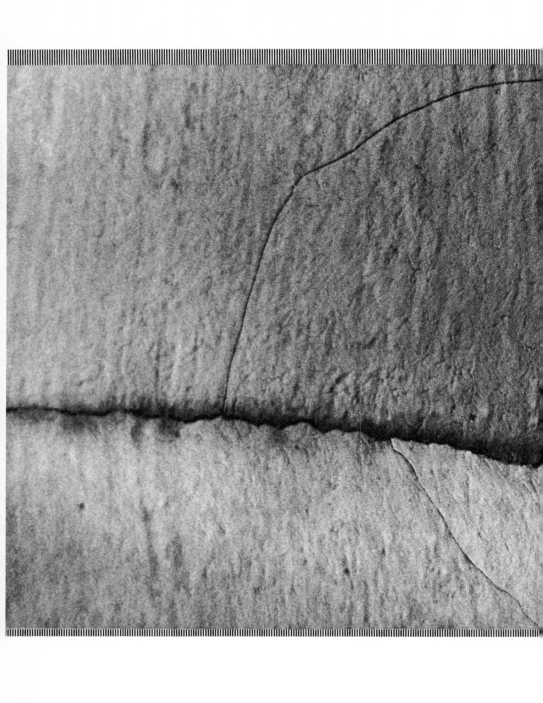

A SCREAMING WHISPER

Poems by
Vanessa Howard

Photographs by
J. Pinderhughes

HOLT, RINEHART AND WINSTON New York, Chicago, San Francisco

A number of the poems in this book
originally appeared in *The Voice of
The Children* Weekly, published by
The Voice of the Children, Inc.

Copyright © 1968, 1969, 1970, 1971 by
        The Voice of the Children, Inc.
Copyright © 1972 by Vanessa Howard

Published simultaneously in Canada by
Holt, Rinehart and Winston of Canada, Limited
ISBN: 0-03-091303-9 (Trade)
ISBN: 0-03-091304-7 (HLE)
Library of Congress Catalog Card Number: 79-182781

Printed in the United States of America
First Edition

Designed by Aileen Friedman

**To my Mother
and Father
with deepest love
and to my best friend, Michael Gill**

Special thanks to Terrill Bush, Anna Winand, June Jordan, and to all my friends and The Voice of the Children.

CONTENTS

PREFACE

Poetry to me is another way of life, one that never ceases. A word is eternal even when forgotten and a poem is everlasting. Poems sometimes take the place of medicines, talks, hatred, violence, anger, pain, love or tears, preserving beautiful moments and easing bad ones. In writing my poetry, I have tried to capture all that fascinates me, contain all that's beautiful, restore all that's destroyed, and soothe all that's painful.

And
still
we
live
on...

Praise the rat-infested rooftop
a jive time junkies paradise
Worship broken bulbless hallways
a winoes wonderland
                    and
Communism
Socialism
Radicalism
Capitalism
Nationalism all the isms isn gettin me

anywhere,
            but right back here
                        again to say
America the Great
America the Mighty
America the Beautiful
                    Say Whaaaaaaaat? □

America
an overdeveloped
        animosity stamping out the dreams
that come from sleepless nights.
Figuring out new types of sin
        practically no progress,
call for the constant cliché
        let's try again.

America
    a whirlpool of waits—
wait till taxes total all you own
wait till space ships supposed to carry you
        are gone
wait till old age wisely wipes out waiting.

America
    more polluted than its airs or seas
    suddenly aware time is not standing still
    till . . . □

GIFTS OF AMERICA

The vacant lots abundant with debris
I take as gifts of America to me
I do not wait for Christmas or birthdays to come around
But presents are all over, even on the grounds.

The buildings are gifts, even torn and old
the hallways and rooms even crude and cold,
the playgrounds even empty, deprived of children's voices
the children's dead careers deprived of any choices
hatred and scorn and dirt
tears and pain and hurt
they come to me
all free
gifts of America to me. □

AFTER THE RAIN

After the rain I walk in the meadow
thinking how free and fresh it is
opposed to a ghetto
thinking of the tall trees that drink
the fallen rain
thinking of the tall buildings where
poverty cries in pain
A field stretching out endlessly on
and on without a gate
a ghetto people trapped inside
trapped by poverty, greed and hate
After the rain I walk in the meadow
with ill feelings left behind
for the ghetto is all those who dwell in it
but the meadow alone is mine. □

Don't tell me you don't understand
                              undecided
                              unable
unwilling is the word
won't educate my children
won't give them jobs without an education
don't understand an urban problem
a so called somewhere slum
what leaky ceiling?
what broken faucet?
what godless ghetto bum?

Don't tell me you don't understand
wishfully thinking as you will,
cause rat ruled buildings reign this earth
and even the White House
                              got roaches. □

The silent city cries today
aware always of the unexpected
crouching in fear of what might
never be
or what might be all too soon
they know, these tall towering buildings
that they will shatter and fall
under the might of what
might be.
How can I explain the unexplainable
predict the unpredictable
or determine when death shall catch us
unaware
in the robes of
war. □

Agnew rushes into the waiting room
where ghetto dwellers have been waiting all their
lives
while Nixon lies D.O.A.
from an overdose of poverty and taxation
and still
      we
         live
           on. □

Cars screech, sirens roar with discontentment
while disenchanted bodies
lurk the streets with faces fitted for sadness.
In times like these
                    when the whole world seems at a
stark raving standstill
it sometimes seems best just to sit and
stare. □

I never heard of no ghetto gardens

MONUMENT IN BLACK

Put my Black father on the penny
let him smile at me on the silver dime
put my mother on the dollar
for they've suffered for more than
three eternities of time
and all money can't repay.

Make a monument of my grandfather
let him stand in Washington
for he's suffered more than
three light years
standing idle in the dark
hero of wars that weren't begun.

Name a holiday for my brother
on a sunny day peaceful and warm
for he's fighting for freedom he
won't be granted
all my Black brothers in Vietnam
resting idle in unkept graves. □

VICTIMS OF SLAVERY

Chained to iron
I am not free
as for the cotton
it's all I can see
Chained by society
caught in hate and
do's and don'ts
Black and Beautiful?
Yet who is it that said to me
the most beautiful things in
life are free. . . . □

THE NEW MATH

White plus White equals one
one race group in size
Black plus Black equals none
we are not recognized
This was the New Math taught to us,
and this too was the sum
that Black and Black equals nothing
but White and White are one
But we could not accept this
and times them both by three,
and found if the world tried hard enough
together they equaled unity.
But the teacher said this could not be,
If Hate remained the hero
and if fighting continued on,
Soon Black and White would equal
zero □

i am frightened that
the flame of hate
will burn me
will scorch my pride
scar my heart
it will burn and i
cannot put it out.
i cannot call the fire department
and they cannot put out the fire within my soul
i am frightened that the flame of
hate will burn me
if it does
i will die □

TO THE NATURE LOVERS

Through the dirt on my windows
it is sometimes difficult to
                relate to the sun
and I can't exactly dig grass
                rolled up in a piece of paper
and I guess water's not so beautiful
coming from a running faucet
                and I never heard of no
                ghetto gardens □

DEAD END KIDS

We Black dead end kids
striving struggling to win identity
reaching for a star that is not there
a star that will not be there nor will it appear
a star that shines over the white child's head,
the white child's house and the white child's bed

We Black dead end kids
trying to get through this life
trying to walk these white paved roads
Only to meet a dead end
with no destination □

NATURAL ARUBA

Naturalism
            is easier
                        than playing games
                        with one's identity
here yesterday
            gone today
                        back again
                                    tomorrow.
Stop going through changes
never being yourself
                        except on rainy days
                        or days you decide to
                                    stay in the house.
Some people die unreal
never ever knowing
                        naturalism
                                    as the reason for living
the cause
            cause
to be truly free is not
                        being what you want to be
but
      being what you are. □

FOR MY CHILDREN

My children are Unique
They are not animated ill-created
figments of someone else's imagination
in disguise

They are not inhumane, profane, or insane
with bottles in their mouths
and America on the brain
my children are wise

My children are live
they are not little doll girls or boys
or battery powered toys
that stand around in corners waiting
for new games

They are not story book characters
from forgotten fairy tales
or Mrs. So and So's children
my children have names

My children are me
They are not images of tomorrow
or shadows of yesterday
or miniature stoney statues
my children feel

And of all the children
in the world, they
are the best to me
ever growing in their blackness
ever striving to be real. □

Jesus Christ can you justify
just what's happening to me
Can Peter Paul and Mary do something
beside sing folksongs
Will St. John pay the rent this week
and I'll be in church on Sunday,
evening service on Monday
Will some righteous holy-holly saint save the
sinner from the day
are you listening
do you hear me
Hey God! □

WE DISAPPEAR TO DANCE

Black we are
we disappear to dance
in the shadows
to play
to listen to jazz
to dig soul
to dig LeRoi Jones
Nina Simone
Aretha Franklin

Black that we are
we disappear and stay.
White that they are
they wish we'd
disappear
for GOOD. □

We have had
              stand ins
              sit ins
              walk ins
              talk ins
              lie ins
and even
              die ins
and still
              we are out of it. □

Yesterday while walking down
the avenue
        I saw a group of Emancipated Negroes
claiming they were free
and while looking I nearly broke
                                my neck
tripping over their chains. □

Consciously I understand
my constant crushing world

He stood a tall silhouette of love
                    beautifully structured
to the soul of his core
deep dark brown a skin
                    lips lying longing to be kissed
hands that seem made to hold another
eyes echoing the reason for giving love
                    and the need for accepting
in the hollows of my mind
                    mentally minding another's
                                world
reaching out I realized
            that he was
                    mine. □

Your eyes like cups of wine
they seem so far away
while drawing closer
I held your hand still cold
I loved you with a heart of stone
which
      crumbled
           after
               every
                  kiss. □

my thoughts are i love you
or do i really?
we talk of dreams, wonderlands,
sugar coated problems,
candy castles.
of times where john always loves mary
but never much of reality
where are the vibrations of love
i should feel for you?
i feel as though i've lost something never possessed
in a whirlpool of undivided emotions
i have penetrated through the barrier of your soul
and you have not pierced the skin of mine
why?
why am I still holding back
existing with a fear locked inside
and no duplicate keys are made
you and i one
        yet always two
never really coming together
              in reality. □

dark so dark
      little light little sense of reality
or knowing anything real.
      coming closer
          together together
crying cause i love you
      loving me
        with pain
dying from love from you
kissing me it burns still
        within
without
    tension
      growing strongly weak
then
   relief
     satisfaction
      release
welding together, thick in the satisfaction
of your desire.
my body wrapped in yours,
finally together,
    one. □

The night is beautiful
i lie with you
        wrapped in the comfort of
                my breast
covered with love in our nudity
holding you holding me
            so close
tender lips soft smooth
            still in love

the night is beautiful
        till i awake
        and find you were never
                there □

Caressing caresses
I awake to the touch
of your lips on mine
while the sun reflects
my eyes in yours
making images of our
tomorrow today
slowly sleep leaves me
sneaking quietly away
and the city sounds
outside greet me hostilely
but I have you to keep the calm . . . □

Subconsciously
        I think of you
              when times were good
      but
consciously
       I understand my
           constant
              crushing
                world. □

A POEM FOR MICHAEL

Day fades into night
sound into silence
and I into you
          things seem calm now.
When I think of leaving you
I hold tighter
kiss harder
I feel sadder.
        But when I think of
        coming home again,
Love bursts into a thousand minutes,
giving us,
      more
        time. □

Calmness hits the careless streets
where strangers stride seeking already sought for
horizons
winds that do not whisper at all like the poets
say
soft spoken shadows hiding happily sad
and I walk watching wishful for forgotten times
in places where our souls
                    linger
                         longer. □

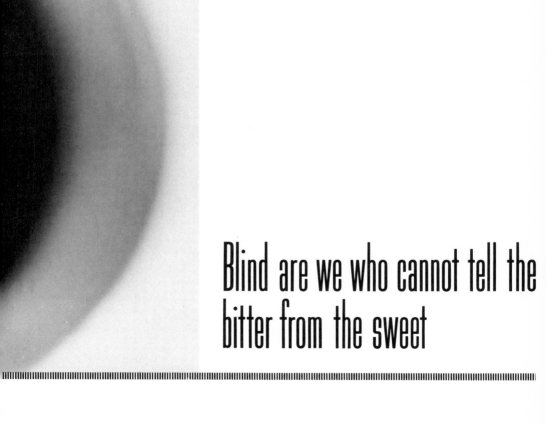

Blind are we who cannot tell the bitter from the sweet

LIFE IS A TWO-WAY EXPERIENCE

Twist spinning
            into love
go running out
            of hate
back into
            loneliness
and stretch into
                trust
but if you can't
            make it
                or just
                    can't take it
remember life
            is a two-way
                    experience
one way is living
        the other is dying
it's your choice
            either way
                you lose ☐

Blind are we who cannot tell the
bitter from the sweet
existing simultaneously not at all
reaching for the pre-existing past in pleasure
and pain
while lives continue living dead
we see the world tomorrow turning into today
                                    sweetly bitter
                                    bitterly sweet   □

In the sweetness of silent death
we sometimes miss the feeling of never awaking. □

In the misty hollow of the morning
dewdrops dance upon the glass and
blades of grass
simply the sun comes, something only
routine
while sounds break the air
to greet you in the pathway
another day begun
and grandma still sits in the window
waiting patiently
for death. □

FOR MY GRANDPA

If anything seemed unreal,
it was you lying still,
                    motionless
with no funny jokes to tell
or faces to make,
the Preacher talked but they
could never sum you up
                    in words
and neither could I
so I'll write a poem in your image
and while others fix you
on their minds, in your coffin,
                    while they cried
I remembered you the way
you were,
        happy,
                and gentle
before you died. □

ABANDONED

She had on sandals
       and a scarf around her head
and her skin was brown from
       daily toil
she seemed to me to kiss the trees
and beckon the flowers from
       the soil
once in a while her tears would fall
       but they fell gently like the rain
she always tried to show a smile
       even in sadness
       even in pain
I watched her working in the fields
       sometimes singing
       Gospel tunes
She worked until the end of day
       across the sky would fly
       the moon
As I watched them working there
       in a line one after another
Sometimes I'd shake her by the arm
       and question her, "Are you my mother?" □

What uncaring creator on this earth
makes one become
                a bum
living life day to day
with no expectance for tomorrow
no acceptance from the world
who creates these soil stained clothes
as unclean as the soul who wears them
in no need or want for purification
happiness an empty hallway or alleyway
or any way out of the way of the world
where those of us who turn our nose up at him
dwell
not because of his filth
or ungodliness in his way
but knowing with disgust
                that we are his creator □

Carelessly
wet rain falls upon the pillow of the
undesired
existing in a world lackful of
feeling
and so shall they weep
                  harvesting only
                  sorrow
                  that needs no care nor
                  cultivation
                  reaping only
                  pain
that comes and goes of its own will
and still
they are the undesirable undesired
and so shall they weep. □

The corner coffee klatch begins,
but wine bottles be they cups
they build a fire and aromas mix sweetly
                          with the air
                              gypsy rose
                          still they favorite
                              pick me up.
This group of forgotten humans
find it easy to smile upon the world
in the situation it is today
totally
disorganized, disillusioned and disabled
empty wine bottles be they only worries
it lasting least of all for ever.
A place to sleep more pleasing than the political
candidates for next year
they sleep soundless except for the
snoring South Pacific brings
and occasionally they smile
admiringly
            at the
                not
              so
              Virgin
                Mary. □

He lay in the alley
                    dead, cold
his helmet lay beside
                    him
his gun in his hand still
                    hot from firing
his badge not so
                    shiny now
and his face still had
                    that expression of
                    surprise □

OBSERVATIONS ON A SUBWAY TRAIN

People just ain't for real
like the man on the train who purposely steps on my toe,
so I can see his imitation, imitation alligator shoes,
so old they're snapping back at me.
Like the stone faces, not really stone at all.
Like the people who get thrills out of looking out
the front of underground trains
watching endless tracks of tracks of tracks and
tracks and more tracks.
Faggots who ain't even funny
like platinum wigs and fluorescent bras,
and retarded people actin' wise
while wise people act retarded
and the old lady with sneakers and anklets
displaying her mountainous and bumpy legs

Is it possible to hijack a train to Cuba,
I wonder?
I remember how everybody had on my shoes and
I had on everybody else's,
Each of us knowing the forbidden word, price.
I remember people always lookin' for wrong,
like the girl with short hair: she had to be a butch
or a faggot—can't anybody realize she's just a girl
with short hair?

Some people stare dead at you,
their eyes lookin' you up and down,
others give you those sly side glances.
And the Chinese man who comes on and looks at me sort of
strange, I wonder if he will ask me
can he press my shirt . . .
and still everybody's pushin' and
shovin'.

Then, finally your stop comes
and you emerge from this underground web of confusion,
and you surface to hysteria.
Racin' to the bus
Fightin' for a seat,
funny how people leave the seats in the back for last
but finally I am home and free
'til tomorrow when I again shall
submerge
in madness. □

YESTERDAY

Yesterday the sun shone bright,
over a snow covered hill
yesterday a tender sight
a bird on my window sill.

Yesterday the rivers flowed
cool and clean and free
yesterday it was not cold
and sights were there to see.

Yesterday my heart was happy
my heart was calm and gay
yesterday was wonderful
but now it is today. □

The night seems to
                 cry
like a child
           lost
the sky seems to frown in
                    pain
while the stars seem dimmer than
                            ever
                               before

do they know? □

They took away the
windmill and the
sailboat too
and the wind was
idle with nothing to do
nothing to do but to
roam aimlessly
desolate   abandoned
forgotten, like me. □

ACKNOWLEDGMENT

Acknowledging that life's purposes
are not fulfilling until fulfilled
at one time or another
Acknowledging that in the birth of my soul
lies a new nation
that waits to be born
Acknowledging that love is not all happiness
and happiness is not all love,
that life is what you make it, when you make it
if you can
Acknowledging when you look at me you see
a love supreme
that i am a purpose in your life now,
revolving around your internal being
Acknowledging all these things,
                 in the time it took for me to grow
in the time it took for me to know
to visualize
to fantasize
but finally to realize
                 I am a woman. □

INDEX TO FIRST LINES

About the Author

Vanessa Howard was born in 1955, in Brooklyn, New York. She began writing seriously at the age of twelve when she joined The Voice of the Children, a creative-writing workshop. Several of her poems received high critical praise when they were published in the anthology *The Voice of the Children.* At present Miss Howard attends the Williston-Northampton Academy in East-hampton, Massachusetts. In addition to poetry, she is especially interested in music and working with young children. She says that her goals in life are to become a literature teacher and a writer.

Of the poems in *A Screaming Whisper,* Miss Howard says: "They are about many things, but mainly all things that should be changed, all things that should be recognized, all things that should be done. Actually I have been writing and living them all my life, but just now they are being made known to the public. I have written this book mainly because of the need for these things to be known and the need for all to listen and hear, but mostly to understand."

About the Artist

J. Pinderhughes is a free-lance photographer who lives in New York City. He attended Howard University and the National Educational Television Film Training School, and has traveled in Ethiopia, Kenya and Mexico.

In connection with his photography for this book, Mr. Pinderhughes says: "I sat down and I read through the poems and I let the natural 'vibes' of the poems strike me. In doing so, they found a home within my own experiences and it was at that point that I began to conceptualize the visual materials. For me it was not a difficult task because Vanessa and I have a great deal in common, the difference being that she writes what she feels and I show it photographically. Film is my medium, communication is my end."